Hologrammatical

Hologrammatical
Poems 2012 - 2022

Philip Salom

PUNCHER & WATTMANN

First published in 2023
Published by Puncher and Wattmann
PO Box 279
Waratah NSW 2298

http://www.puncherandwattmann.com

puncherandwattmann@bigpond.com

NATIONAL
LIBRARY
OF AUSTRALIA

A catalogue entry for this book is available from the National Library of Australia.

ISBN 9781922571946

Cover image 'Hologram Flow' sequence by YouWorkForThem (www.you-workforthem.com)
Cover design by Miranda Douglas
Printed by Lightning Source International

Contents

Hologrammatical

Inside the darkness
underneath the light
sits over me and

I waited for years
a cone of awareness
never once moves off

I dreamt this and when it returns it makes
sense if no matter what I look for in my life
more remains unseen, more never happens.

Inside the cone of light
always of the darkness
like any normal person

I feel myself aware
as I eat and I drink
the tunnel lifts to a peak

As a child I dreamt of a single clenched fist
moving through space towards me with frightening
malevolence. I would wake before it reached.

Cause and effect may
taking years decades even
erratically. Where is it?

be indolent a union
changing location
Can I trust the future?

A peak and a band of light is moving level to vertical
like a torch beam or a searchlight above a city
during war or up there in the branches - an owl.

I see Bosch's spiky souls
to that tunnel of light
What happens next?

rising like little glassy eels
punctured in the dark
Don't believe them.

Via Negativa, perhaps. The future is hologrammatical:
re-arranging its meaning on the mind's thin chain.
The links, the gaps, the unprovable intuitions.

Operation at the Royal Melbourne

But I can't be there.   I'm still at my desk.
                                     My way of seeing is to close
the blind: I must imagine you.

                                     To permit a report
to give evidence   requires a witness.
To be that witness is to see
in one at least of its metaphors.

To navigate, then, within   and without a vision.

You are watching out for
what you cannot see   under general anaesthetic
within you   leaves you without you.

Surgeon nurse anaesthetist   the sibilant attendance of
people leaning over you white tubes and monitors
begin to devour you.

You will make landfall.   I know it. I would travel
beside you but I am witness of a different sort.
The cliches are reassuring.

At the beginning and the end
of operations, is a loss   of self to ritual.
Eyes closed you will be shifting.

What is it shimmers in   the mind's tiny chambers
like a hologram?   Its poor reception.

This is not a report.
This is a translation.

Not being Lazarus

Doctor, nurse, gadgetry.
He marks my bare back
pushes into me a steel
probe like a bike spoke
one inch or three ...
no anaesthetic for this.
Pulls it out like a long
silver gasp and pushes
it in again with a twist.
It is wired up to a box
of dials and messages,
a screen that crackles
like hysterical birds
white cold in the wind.
Eight in and seven out.

I rest for seconds then
above my skin he shifts
down (or across?) to jab
again in the pain. No, it
isn't that pain so much
as having to push and
brace against his push
so the steel cannot miss
me forced into a corner
and skewered precisely.

I feel of feeling hideous.
Sleep Palsy, he tells me.
Derelicts get it, paralytic,
sleeping on pavements.
Saturday night Palsy.
Sheaths on the nerve
wrecked. *Do you want*
to lie down? People faint
or fall over about now.
Oh, dumb flâneur...

The static is crackling
just off all my stations.
The louder the static
the less is happening.
I've never seen it as bad
as this. Then a joke
which I miss but not
ten more insertions
as a colleague enters
and wants to see this
oddity I am. A screen
reads me as a wall of
noise. The white face

of God? But I feel
more like the son.
There's no soul here,
the specialist says
(overtrained atheist).
Samuel Beckett's
more desolate plays?
So I confess I slept
drunk on her futon
until this white fuse
went off in my neck
pattern-blast of pain
like neon billboards.
The axon murders!
Now I cannot sleep,
lit up like an addict
without a rush, my
pain like an animal
tracked into my
shoulder and shot.

After two months I
feel but cannot lift
my hand up to point
to a bird in the sky
or for long enough
for anyone to see it.

And a third month:
in the shower I feel
the shoulder bone
thin as a handrail
and turn suddenly
to the mirror: two
whole muscle-groups
have collapsed.

I wait at the lift
with six other people,
then a dozen, we wait
ages as twenty of us
now stand there,
all sick in some way.
Some the breasts,
the lungs, the cancers.
The lift is huge by
the look of its doors.
Our illnesses are wide.
Two dozen of us.
And the smell
of flowers.

Am tired am not homesick

a proliferation of shark's teeth

a short phrase is less vulnerable

beauty lacking but not too long

but first tell me what you want

each night each word is slower

more than a Buddhist admits

you mustn't gatecrash the truth

a car turning into a side-street

it won't get you anywhere

a tiny amount is just too much

of otherness: life has orphaned

we are vulnerable we long

lets my wings furl and unfurl

a sentence is filling with blood

but may engage a border limit

sky is cheerless long and black

reach over me if you kiss her

it is succulent as a narrative

each table is set with knives

if it hurts her it will be finished

and yes her leg is ergonomic

and his mind is homeopathic

let the blood come longing

ultimately we lose oh fair shark

if a poem if teeth if a sentence

so tired but not homesick

Time and Motion Study: Nesting

You were told: It's not God, it's chance. And chance is ? Don't say everything
happens for a reason. The world is particularly dispassionate?
School-days — his legs clinking
a polio boy stamped in splints
like the gunslinger in his spurs
stepping up onto the wooden
verandah boards and opening
his lunch box. He knew pains
we didn't so we mocked him.
Squinting behind glasses, plain
Italian in a town Anglo-Saxon
C of E, our agnostic religions.
Chance-hobbled, but he lived.

You saw men walking in hesitation, splints invisible. And the legs'
disproportion, wheelchair-rowing shoulders, their power, their pain.
Our cousin the egg-stealer
genius shimmied up trees:
his arms and legs spidering
trunks, out along branches,
egg seller for kid collectors.
He fell, the one time time
waits for. The splints in his
neck broke inside-out - as
bone-bare - and like death
the tiny egg he reached for,
its sky-blue speckled shell
clutched in his right hand.

You considered Fate as a thought, the black gap behind accident or car
crash, to explain the deaths of brothers, how it was ever possible:
my best friend's beloved cousin
dragged from a car-wreck onto
the road, was then run down by
an ambulance howling to hospital.
His other cousin crushed by a milk
carriage on sliprails to the pick-up.
The policeman's son reported the
mother of the big boy in year six
had hung herself, in their garage,
among oil drums and spider webs.

You had played there just months before. She had brought sandwiches, and
nothing in her face. You never went back, you couldn't go back.
Knowing nothing we imagined
her long floral dresses, vertical
and still, and like her wardrobe,
her standing inside its shadows.
Not knowing how any mother
could, or look like, hanged, and
still did not when a teenage boy
did it. Whether it was different.

In paralytic images you hallucinated in your innocent or blank minds.
Angels didn't visit agnostics, the only *actual* angels stood in marble:
in the Catholic cemetery. One
photo of the dead to remind
them so they could flap out
free of their hard bodies to be
full of light to those we knew
who'd slipped outside to die.
Those who saw, or never saw
a life ending, death in the nest.

Tell me what your mother said. You had to live with his death inside
your once entirely innocent body. She thought there had to be a reason.
For years after he had died
my mother said: *your brother*
is in heaven. If there is love
it's that close, and that far
away. My eyes said: *wait for*
me to blink. (As some of us
have seen death, close up,
we're different.) We never
asked, and no one ever said -
nothing could be changed.

Time and Motion Study: the Universe

It's the long gentle snoring of a motorbike
the sound coming through my open window
like evidence of ordinary life.

       Then lost in life's silence.

The suburbs are set out like a calendar,
all the days at once, but I am one blank square
on a blank page. Filling one page is enough.

I don't believe a calendar of worm-holes
or multiples universes. Such a waste of time,
literally, to say nothing of resources.

Do I want to hear the sound of a real
or a metaphorical motorbike diminishing
with the universe into another Universe?

I can't predict the future. Live the already lived?
Pretending I can or imagining I can is a form
of preparedness, like the Stoics' equanimity.

But it's odd when you think about it: when
about the future we're almost always wrong.
That almost being the gambler's addiction.

From the window I can almost see the sun
setting into the ocean like a wind blowing
through the coals of a forge. Then out there

in the universe, diminishing.

Time and Motion Study: the Accident

That day I drive a hundred gravelly corners
sideways, surfaces churning, uphill downhill
into a closing radius, corners like corkscrews.
Driving in feel like moving on my own track
as if it's foreseen, decided, ahead of the fact.

Until one as I somehow travel out of time,
returning as the car pitches and barrel rolls
inside the strange darkness of a solar eclipse.
Slowly. Then seeing and feeling the car leap
reversing into the light, up-righting itself to
lunge through the wire fence of a paddock,
like a bull.

      A dozen cows thunder towards
us, me, my passenger, our utter transport.
Their dark eyes have not seen this before,
we were not as other creatures sitting up:
this green car with its sides shoved in, its
right headlight hanging loose like the eye
of an animal that's been shot. Of nothing
moving. What could cattle see in our eyes'
front and rear vision pulled wide and huge
by fear?

      Now I recall I had asked my mate:
Are you alright? no, *not then*, but as the car
razed the gravel shoulder, as we had pitched
off the road, that crazily I had kept one hand
on the wheel, one on the flimsy door handle,
as if my accident had finished before it began.
I don't recall his answer. Or he said nothing
until we were stalled, fence wire tangled up
underneath, a green car ten metres into this

welcome paddock of slow clover and cows.
I drove back onto the road, remembering
at least the right order of things, before I
like a good country boy repaired the fence
with farm-boy adrenaline fingers at speed
until this routine calmed me, as if the wire
bent easily into the problem of fencing up
with figure-eight knots the boundary I had
broken through, but returned him from.
Each breath tied down, pulled tight until
I studied the fence line.

    It just wasn't straight.

Ode to Slow Water

Watching your slopes of river
lessens the fast art of humans.
To swim in you is to enter
your grace in your slowing
movements you carry and carry
us into yourself like dreaming.

*

Gentle enough today to calm my
breathing, your gentle washing through
caries of granite, teeth in the stoneface
your tongue is probing loose
after centuries.
If I bend down closely at the fall
I can hear this work of yours
beyond knowing.

*

In being always not yourself
you have no time to think.
I watch you ever replaced
by your own body and shape.

*

You have no head, river, no limbs, no organs,
but fullness. You show how cumbersome I am.
I watch you elemental, in passing into an otherness
of speed: you are like births and deaths per second.

*

You cannot see you are immortal.
You trickle through your centuries as if
ours never happened.

When you sift the sedimentary layers
of us, we do not.
But now your waters are hot
until they cease
and now our centuries have used you up
and then destroyed you.

*

We are disfluent, you are chthonic.
If left to ourselves we are
unreliable: beings of gabion
uptightly, jostling. And ...
we are the lords of evaporation.

Coda to Slow Water

You pour one glass full of clear spirit
into a second glass. You pour it back.

Slowly, for the rest of the day you pour
it one way, then back, glass into glass.

Full into empty, emptying as emptiness
fully. Until doing this for long enough

nothing is left. Your clear spirit is clear.
Saying: I did this. Stating you did this.

Out of something, out of its purpose
calling it progress. Or two empty glasses.

Turns of the Screw: an Ode

You talk like Southern slang or a 747 at take-off: volume not
aliens. The sky is funnelling through your blown speakers.
You're relentless but mindless you are probably Republican.
Balanced on Imbalance maker of cliches
your air-vase spins faster than the earth spins
elephant-coloured and hesitant as a lover
letting down your
trunk

Anti-gravity you unravel the houses and suction
the parts: your ID surfaces churn on the screen
like a vicious 3D modelling you hate
outlines your shapes and pixels
are ripping off the picture
like Escher's Rind.
Inhuman face of
the subject
us

Cruel lover. You jilt us into a hundred trees in spasm
buildings blowing their brains out as undone barns
erupt in gyres their loose hay turning to swarm
cars drive up walls and frantic things
lose their minds sheds and even
our houses are interbreeding
are mounting other houses
to copulate and die
in pieces.

Because children are crazy about you they are as stunned
　　　　as the dust. A hundred metres up dairy cows are circling
　　　　　　the airy rotolactor three hours before milking time.
　　　　　　　　　　You as and your making us as if (but where are we?)
　　　　　　You suck a row of houses and spit the verandahs.
　　　　　You are alive as the opposite fact of us but you
　　　　　　are awe: somehow you open us
　　　　　　　　out of a greyish
　　　　　　　　　　nowhere we are
　　　　　　　　　　　staring.

Staring, not learning. You are weather winding off the pattern. After your
velodrome of an afternoon your race falls crashing onto roads. Odd dogs that
cannot sit and doors and a person with a sheep and window frames and a
baby planted like a mandrake in a field. What they don't know yet is all your
world falling in us particle and wave a lifetime flung to quanta. More and
more often. In trouble. From you and your bloodshot I.

Weather Presentation?

Weather comes out of the presenter's finger
and dies.
It's dead again the following night.
It's dead on arrival, this weather.
This is a mortality reality TV show.
Weather presenters dress like undertakers
but try to be characters,
and jokey:
Weather, get a life! Or change your friends.

Weather falling on paddocks is agricultural,
but falling on flood plains is not accidental
yet politicians deny
they denied not only the phrase *flood plain*
they deny that weather is even climate.
It surprises them in every interview,
and the weather presenters
try so hard
dying every night to tell them.

Captain oh my *Captains*

These people don't believe in war deep
down they just invest in industries that
make them work. Like war was a chart
or a spreadsheet, the blood and
the screaming in a different building.

Like they don't believe in
climate change they cannot make a profit from.
Are we so shallow we can't do
something awful to them in exchange? Call it
a business transaction, to do it best nothing
like a conscience needed.

I suggest: plant them neck deep in the desert
tie them to the first floor above a flood plain
in boardrooms let them breathe their
paid-for fumes and the CO_2 they are
responsible for.
Because it is another war and war's investments.
If they complain do not believe them.
If they try to buy their way out
render them as bankrupt as they've always been
morally.
Tell them telling lies makes people violent
and believing lies makes people violent
and knowing you're being lied to, ditto.
So here they are the tellers being told. Or
amplify angry unsubtle poetry into their bedrooms
every night until they scream.
Then tell them 97% of scientists
cannot hear them.

Go On Then, Deny It

Drought. The shipwrecks of sheep and cattle
Delacroix hulls and rafts in the ocean of dust.

In the city no citizen has butchered anything
to eat it. Governments and truth come close.

Lost opportunities are the worst
and they cost us everything. At the time ...

But: the shelf life, Antarctic ice collapsing like
a modulation in Beethoven (he could not imagine).

Paraquat or genotoxins, the surface of the world
eats us from the inside, we are its climate change.

As I wrote this the government denied it. It claims
full expertise (government change is what worries it).

The moon is out and *is* full. I hate Conservatives
how they align the lying arts, the naked capitals.

Then fires came. Then floods came. Came again.
He is on his iPhone. The town floats by on a bed.

Augean

So here we are back in the Augean stables
our dung-house of hypocrites and liars.

But now it isn't Classical it's Literal:
not pouring the river into the stable

but pouring the sewage into the river.
80 million people voted for the Tories.

73 million people for the US Narcissist
who hated them. Every day the world

watched media for how these sociopaths
didn't care. They are hypnotically awful.

The floods they don't believe is change
can't wash their shit away, and people if

not cattle, can know a stable is unstable
when leaders believe in God yet they are

shitting everywhere until their freaky Rapture
seizes their heads from their arseholes.

Time is shuffling cards across the sky. Our
Labours. We left one day to clean this up?

Pessimism as a Dream

Ficus trees have grown inside our house.
My son climbs up to knock the football down
we kicked into the over-hanging branch ...
We're playing football in the kitchen
on slate that reminds me of the dead
laid beneath the floor-stones of cathedrals,
stain-glass breaking up the light.

Outside, light flays the bush like nine-tails
so glarily the shock of looking out
reminds me of my dangerous driving as a youth
half-drunk, half-mad, half-blinded
by ultra-violet scatter from wet roadways.
Now it's CO_2, methane, lack of ozone above us.

I fear for my son until he's down,
remembering a boy who fell from nesting, who crept
along the branches for the eggs and slipped,
his spine jutting like an up-you fingers from his neck.
We play until it rains onto our furniture —
that's the cost of having trees inside.

I cook dinner, dodging and hand-shy
among electrical machines so utterly drenched
they could kill me any minute. Even that.
I've heard it once-removed, from articles
of women dying foot-white at the washing,
and spinning. It's safer for our neighbours
swimming naked in our lounge-pool, pale
as the fashion, now the atmosphere's broken.

Depressed, I wander in to watch them.
They are not sexy nor great nor great at sex
I guess, but who knows? I've never asked them.
They just swim. There's a blemish in the air above us.
The daylight dims. Then you rub up behind me.
You gave me the pessimism test, once, and
I passed it, with failing colours: that is, I am.

Sometimes, quite simply, I want to scream.

The Weather Fugues

Loss

Blind from the kitchen table where they ate their meals
it emerges eyes open and unexpected in him forty years

later than the fourteen and a half thousand times the world
has spun: his father gone his brother gone his old mother

gone his other brother brought close, then let walk back,
deaf on the water. These. And now the weather watcher

turns the pages down like a tent and checks the internet
for storms and graphs his favourite site the interpreter

of data. Making slow figures into still graphs that flash
in his mind. People had thought the clouds and sunlight

work of the will, and were God's symbols or God's tricks
doing their duty. If the seasons stood in fours like elders

weather was sudden history, weather the mess your life
was strewn by, weather was picky and ferocious. Then

we... brought it in: it was nothing more or less than us.
Its death is moving back in us, not ours to understand:

tsunamis cyclones flooding fire and the many thousands
dead we have no words for, but the silence when belief

grinds to standstill. Watching doesn't help but it returns
to a child his father tapping the glass of the barometer.

Which gods were they, altering the air and the goodness:
preceding, being, following, around us as we walked out?

Change

Outrageous destruction the paddocks he ploughed the flats
he planted the trees in swaying lines like hurrahs by Robert

Frost, kazoos by Wallace Stevens, poetry does not belong here
when the evil farms of finance arc-out the soil like electricity

collusion persuasion the rhetoric of poisoned land-form here
not there was mention made of men women Indigenous hands

no not likely. Carbon trading here is the sad deal so a rockface
shatters in aesthetic plumes ah wheels and ore trucks raw auras

halo the late night news the Ords Ordinary aflame with birds!
Weather as climate The fire begs you to put it out, as molten

iron seeks the cooling river of death. It will retreat unto gods
who crave destruction of the kind all CEOs can understand

payout payout if the world is fucked then money won't help it.
Take it home, look after it. Our baby. Not your personal profit.

Childhood

Only Sundays hurt and that was any kind of weather
after 3pm when daylight stalled in thoughts of Monday

when clouds were deep in melancholy not delusion not
fear though a small fear of the new day of old routine

was a paradox I couldn't stand repeating.
Nothing I could do brought Saturday back

or even Sunday morning into warmth
and all these years later this transference comes

as she stands against the window sighing, or irons
Monday's collar onto Sunday evening,

the hiss of steam, the queasy smell
of spray under metal.

Discarded Dresser, and Boots

For DM and BM

A ghost: a white-painted dresser with a wooden top
stood just inside the door of the old farm bedroom.

In forced modesty, lost in silence like a mere shelf
for dropped items, this pale twin and lesser-dresser

of its better in the make-up corner: ebony, majestic
mirrors and three drawers under a cool marble top.

Years later, on the verandah, further removed the old
dresser sits under a coverlet of dust, a wing-mirror

lost. When the son and daughter-in-law moved
down the generation of the farm. Coat-rack heavy

and two pairs of rubber boots in wait, for the legs
and steadying paces of routine through the cold,

into frosty paddocks in their hemstitch footprints,
under high level air stranger than words and talk,

more brilliantly known than with words and talk.
In *you* then, working until your hands broke open

in front of you, shovelling the gold of afternoons.
Ice in winter white, the sharp, the dingo of saliva,

the flat, frost abstracts, these airy clouds in you cast
out. (At times we touch the world only as it lets us.)

Then back. Kicked off against the wall like stand-ins:
one pair of boots facing in, and one pair facing out.

Like two people lying in bed, entering hope in the dark.
Their feet a prayer: one pair pointing down, one pair up.

But no children came. There are no names to call them by.
Therefore no answers. The rites of the wheat field failed.

So there's nothing to inherit. Above the house two crows
call out, serious about the weather. They sound like scholars.

It's almost Biblical. And the dresser stands under a coverlet
of ash. Floods and fire passed down. But worse than that.

The Longer Earth

for Meredith

From Carlton North to Carlton walking on Lygon
between the long dead in their final allocations
resigned to the sound of braking or accelerating
trams, and houses facing onto this same pitching
up and down, I think of the strange ways life
is magnified and then reduced, the least and most
magnificent sleep, long considerate of difference.
We walk between, heading towards the city then
turn right to skirt the tall spiked cemetery fence
towards the west, the late sun pretending all is well
as well it may be. As a fine rain tilting downwards
grows on our arms like embroidery. We are alive
and well. If well is what is understood generally,
of the moment, ignoring all else.
Except it's not true. You are desperate for a
better future, you live in the gap between living
and a future of more than any dead can calculate
knowing: heat shrinks and burns equally soft lives
and hard earth, if rain is now relentless, its sound
brings dread. I am not your equal in this. I live on
my nerves and words, my imaginings in present
tense, shorter, particular, varieties of more or less.
Through all the years I have loved the weather
I have trusted time too much. Now the future
rips over the tree tops and the past has settled
in the roots. We walk the longer earth together.

The Future Speaks

You thought the future was slower and forever further off.
It's not.
I tell you, in the future they have one-way vision:
backwards.
It means history is dragged from the past into the present
like resistance.
It reveals how you run the planet backwards and destroy it.
Paradox.
Now the future comes in all directions, it surrounds you with
its argument.
Condition one: For the greatly worried the Golden Age was
in the past.
Condition two: For the monotheists the Golden Time is in
the future.
No one lives in either. Both of these conditions are obsolete.
Listen.
There is less and less time in the future. There will be none.
No cheating.
My mouth moves here and you hear it there. I am the future's
ventriloquist.

Mahler's 2nd (The Resurrection) Symphony and the Ants

Behind the notes' invisible drama is God. Hearing Mahler
as if lunatics and gravity and ants ceaseless as the first
and second movements the strings and a pregnant load
of differing directions, of front and side and pivoting
chords, or of ants unable one at a time to stand still.
Ants as *tendency*, ants as ants in columns on grooves
like dots on CDs the focal movement irrelevant the Sign
and crotchety anywhere of their purpose, their restless
mania for abstraction. No programme notes to read but
then what do Mahler's say — *why do you live? Is it all
a huge joke?* they carry sawn-through leaves as big as
key-signatures, sugar to the living (they rise again)(and again).
No falling back for a cigarette a quick snort a sinus moment
of whisky or cocaine just to keep their fingers and limbs
agitative, the job the job, ants as the minor keys the swell
of doom, ants run onto the track of brassy and timpani
exo-skeletons, in Mahler's grimmest anti-closet yet…
She cries out in heart-stopping anty-mezzo Oh   believe
O glaube es geht dir nicht verlo No, you will not
be lost. And only after the heavy chords, only after
burden-bearing back and forth the difference the diff
-erent and the diffident ants (there have to be some
like us): Die as I shall, so as to live! Who isn't moved
by their famous power-to-weight ratio so very serious
(lift and lift! they lift us up! they are The Resurrection!)
Sterben werd 'ich um zu leben! sings the soprano,
Yes yes and *ja ja* say the ants.

Levitation Elevation

The choir isn't young but it sings flat out
its sound fading on us like afternoon light on old curtains.

Key change, modulation, his tip-of-the-tongue attacks all lost
Pergolesi breaks apart in the vault and falls onto the floor.

A tenor holds his score inches from his face and squints.
The soprano soloist leans back and sings with her breasts

but only the small birds with gullets in her mouth cry out.
The bass is tall and thin and sounds like car doors being shut.

This music flattens on the stands. The lanky-armed conductor
is conducting the air if nothing else the arse-end of his shirt

billowing from his pants and the melody is only kept because
we listen to the music so hard. We want it and the soprano's

cleavage seems to applaud us. All this for the glory of God.
The tenor is using a magnifying glass. The Universe in a breve.

At last the conductor hitches up his pants Pergolesi's legs
swing freely in the vault again: Amen, the music wants

but the choir can't attack the vowel: they sing its heady cons
-onant: ha ha ha ha hamen *pp*   ha ha ha hamen *ff   har menn.*

Music Knows Everything

Because it was his unhappy mind on the keyboard
the music came.

          If there's unhappiness to be had
music wants the first movement or the rock band's
improvising madness.
Thelonious Monk's hat stand
and dancing near the keyboard until his flat hands
bounce on jazz, direct.

          Unhappiness? Music banned it.
Told it to go. Music sat down in its place and played.
It is transference. It sits down as an old fakir stands
and takes in the pain.

          He said the music was so sad
he felt elated. It is old tragedy he wakes from until
gasping with emotion, his legs lift up, his arms bend
down, tight and soft, he feels it coming in.

          Just tidal
or sun-storm. A sun in the middle of our insides,
like its own remote, changing our channels.

          Music does
this, just to know us. Music wants us.

Boy Becoming

It could be that the low-pitched shriek outside
is the boy who never speaks becoming a man.
Of what comes over him as the cold light rain
stands in for his speech, years later, now that is,
he is the person in the shadow of the verandah
who cries and calls to a somewhere he may not
know of, from this place no one can be sure of
until the sunlight soothes in over him by warm
intervals and increments moving up his limbs,
releasing from his body tall now as his father's,
impressions sometimes semi-vocal, expression
uncertain. Eighteen years since we found him
tiny, happy, gazing up into the rain in the dark.
The street looks in and through him in pulses
of light. As if looking for what is looking back.
As if it's true: that any world is a trance of one.

Sitar: Sympathetic Strings for Jayanta
(for Jayanta Mahapatra's 80th birthday)

It's strange the things that readers choose to find.
Your poems have called up Wordsworth in some readers.
There may not be a green shoot or a lake in sight even if
you always stare at water. Water pooling on the red soil.

Your poems have called up Wordsworth in the readers
who want an Indian as a dark-eyed echo of an Englishman
who always stares at water. Water pooling on the red soil.
His inrush of sublime was the child of him in things.

Who wants an Indian as a dark-eyed echo of an Englishman?
Your sad, inner reach was towards the children of Orissa,
his inrush of sublime was the child of him deep in things.
He wanted back his boyhood, and its shining, and its sun.

Your sad, inner reach was towards the children of Orissa.
You who seemed always old, are now an old I searching.
He wanted back his boyhood, and its shining, and its sun.
His made-up other-muse, was Lucy, English and maidenish.

You who seemed always old, are now an old I searching.
You are sad and secular, where he called back endorphins.
His made-up other-muse, was Lucy, English and maidenish.
Yours: ash and blood and violence, the daily living, the dead.

You are sad and secular, where he called back endorphins.
You had seen this all along, saw the undenied, saw it there
in the ash and blood and violence, the daily living, the dead.
Now at eighty the I of you still belongs to this. Not England.

You had seen this all along. You saw the undenied, saw it when
there may not have been a green shoot or a lake in sight. Now
at eighty the I of you still belongs to this. Not England.
It's strange the things that readers choose to find.

Varia of Tattooing

Unlike the public art they liked tattoos: under
their clothes this art of humming not singing,

rituals but private ones, lying under the gun
as it bleeds to become the image and immortal,

signs unlike sounds intermittent in the wind
he said he couldn't tell the difference between,

like a diesel train and a distant plane. Between
harpsichord or organ. A drum or an explosion.

Tattoos were immediate, unmistakeable but muted
from the sun and from the street though if street

tattoos were catching on as art, or from the glam
meaning prison, the jailbird art, the shadow crim

after crimson, green, the blue arts, the aggro arts
for each period of hurt, each given by the artist

forever to them. Here under clothing, humming
from the needle, lurid, are the cliches that cling.

They hoped they'd stay in love, were inclined
to perform mirror-image tattoos side by side.

To make the witticism whole, their front and back
creature of wit: they needed the mirror to see that

on them, of them, their coloured Yin and Yang
their of making love in the blood, knowing it sang

from being so sinuous in their favourite positions,
coming to rest, breathless, humming after singing.

Looking at Literal Blood

He came for me too fast
to react. The side of my palm
opened like two bloody eyelids
under his knife. The eye-shot red.
When he saw the blood he ran.
I stood looking. At this Cyclops.
It bled onto the pavement bled
down my jeans. It told me to sit
on the cold concrete steps.

Years later I trod barefoot on a broken
glass slipper I tried on without looking
too drunk too late at night. From that
bottle came this single-jewel trap
left on the darkened road for a wolf.
I was hard-wired to howl that night.
Howling not singing.
I limped on my left foot
stamping my pawprint in blood.

I was trapped by an intern in casualty.
Three times he shoved the needle in
and three times it bent. Or broke.
No local at my local. His eyes widened
when I said just stitch my foot as it is.
I was drunk. It hurt. I fell back relaxed
by the shocking pain. I
never made it to the ball. Or the forest.

I crashed my bike. Both knees bled.
I looked liked a martyr to praying.
The blood patterned like a Brillo pad
the red clots in long slow threads.
Blood can become a kind of art.
Later I stapled my foot to a rafter
like the original martyr (self inflicted).
Blood has no sense of proportion.

A Vladimir Taxonomy

If his damage is vertical, it rises as floors do
in sidescan TVs and tables, shatterwards of beds
and chequered bedspreads hanging there among
the shrapnel hovering like glass or killer birds.
Then falling into gutters. Oh, people, you'll die.
His imagination is horizontal, it levels everything
reaching to the Tsar, his sense of time is flat.
When he breathes, centuries move backwards.
Most of the time he doesn't. He is impassive,
blanker than a drone above the broken ground.
Raisin-eyed, a man among men (not women)
bare and hairless-chested upon his poor horse
yet a mummy's boy from the first to the last
of his Mother Russia, he was born twice over
into the 20st ... then the 18th Century as well.
A double case of repetition, there is nothing
to *see* in him, he is the enigma of bad acting:
Putin is the personality without a person.
Among their medals: loyalty as much as battle
weighing them down at the far end of the table,
his Generals watch him: cold, pouty as a baby,
yet this terrible, unavoidable vice of his lips.
Immobile he sits there like a dull Villanelle
lobotomised with power: *Glabrous Lobotomous.*

Silly Sonnet

for Mal

Awake for the moment, I turn over and wake
inside this first response of the yet-again night.
Until my second response is checking the time.
This my roll-over habit every night at four am.
Dividing night. Again, I think, again, the first
response keeps telling itself - *it* is the repetition.
Until the second response is checking the time.
Beckett. Nothing to be done. You bastard.
Sleep again. Fail again. Fail better but at
four am. Absurdist insomnia is the worst.
Perhaps the only. It rolls over onto itself
like a mindless double act. Or double option:
lie there doing nothing, or move downstairs
to write this good-for-nothing bloody poem.

The Other Art of Filmmaking

The flies had to be dead because live flies
don't take direction. The prisoner eats them,
which flies won't volunteer for, they don't
understand snuff movies, and spray ads
terrify them. The prisoner in the script is
based on mad English Harker in Dracula
who can sense from bat-scent in the belfry
(what's left of his belfry) that the Count
is on his way. Whereas he only sucks
the little throats of flies.

The film version might just work in fast-cut
shots like a stillness cut up and assembled
into a cubist compound in the brain,
extremity plus technique do much to tame.
He wants the compound insect eye
that sees a hundred fragments and the bat
hearing every brick-and-mortar in the walls.
Yes, he wants God's lunatic endlessness
like the lunatic wants endless flies.

I Step Back Into a Life

on Tuesday... Saturday? Does it matter if I'm wrong? Nothing
can be more oxygenating than waking
on the floor like Dostoevsky. The dizzy disappearing
rain hosing the windows and unexpected sunlight plate-glass
flat-against-the-world remembering
I will surely place onto
or press into the palimpsest the real happening to me.
Yes my own children are living somewhere? laughing at
this same rain and light and cold glare of surfaces
but a different street a different line of trees?
Indoors the furniture the kitchen utensils the clock
on the wall waiting.

Déjà vu is crap. This isn't that. The TV shakes its voice at me.

I lie chest down on what are my cool sheets over-night
to sleep again
where the face of my lover the body of my lover our two
lifetimes of Eros conjoin and wrangle in me
like love and it is love I do not imagine my lover lusting
onstage with a stranger in ventilating gaps of light.
But what is that?
I don't worry at a week's hunger in my nerves or the overcast
mind vertiginous as tripping and falling
twice or stunned by a memory lapse:
seeing once and remembering twice. Resurrection!
Doubt can undo satisfactions
like this. As it should.

The tram has a nervous breakdown in the street.

To breathe is one thing but to live is ambiguous.
I look for I remember familiar things... (can I believe them?)
then see a steel barbecue burning through
the fat of the atmosphere
my two neighbours hacking up their garden
like council shredders then calling for the fire engine.

I walk through the day of the ancient eye with its blue-see
nodular and analogue cruder than a cat's
into the new eye of the me becoming. Becoming
not the middle-eye said to see onto God (oh hello
God so good to see you). Not that.
Difficult getting used to this. The newness the weird bliss.

On the balcony two crows argue about teeth.

Dentistry

His view of it: hidden in my mouth his goggle
and stainless steel reflection, its vertical world.
Goggles for spattering intrusions to the mouth.
Welding in tiny arcs inside the drill holes until
the mine floods: drowning, pumped, drowning.

Reflex 1: Swallowing is involuntary.

Reflex 2: Gagging is embarrassing.

Perhaps music is reflux-free, hearing in the dark
eyes-shut and shutter, trying for dissociation.
No the tools sing in my teeth, the water-level
rises. The gorge. You're doing well, he grins.
Oh the condescending art of the dentist.

Rule 1: Chinese restaurants often get the music wrong.

Rule 2: I try, here, now, to concentrate on any music.

(That Chinese ambient music, is rarely Chinese,
sadly,) My sound-track's a mosquito soprano

the awful high-definition drilling. Blooded. Lost.
My opera: dentistry from underneath is a mouth
with conflict but no stage, not even an audition.

Mouth 1: *Not I*, says the mouth in Beckett's play.

Mouth 2: Inescapably I, gagging. Where else is there to go?

A friend of mine saw this graffiti, said the dentist,
saying: We must save the third world from poetry!
(OGod) Okay. All done. You'll have to come back
next week. Get Sasha to book a new appointment.
So much to do.   Oh fuck.   Once they've got you.

Rule 3: It's never done.

Joshua Slocum and His Dead Reckoning

(in 1898 Joshua Slocum completed the first solo circumnavigation of the world in his sloop the *Spray*)

May: He boiled a tin clock it showed 1896
           8 bells! baked beans every four hours
           The drinking galaxies the dumb bits
           and lumps black puddings and salt

But: Lightning writes longhand on the sky
           the pages so big the sea seems small
           Ol Slocum chants it and loga-rhymes
           circum'd soloing and dead reckoning

May: Using dumb bells his arms are sloops
           rushes of sail-fish are silver leopards
           or the wing-flash of angels unscary
           harbingers he takes inside to see by

Not: Pacific cannibals do not hunt in the
           horse latitudes but by eye and rote
           loga rhythms and little hand drums
           to eat you at sunsets so wearily red

But: Over there into his eyes the horizon
           is jade now and is bleeding a green
           flattened curve of circumnavigation
           the world is too far off to talk of it

May: Super-tankers will sail above themselves
           blind as Manhattan's concrete and steel
           but are not yet invented so the ocean
           can see you the wind is strapped to you

Not: Ten years later Slocum will crank up
           and set spinning a record by the great Caruso
           singing O Paradiso his tenor rising
           from the grooves of the shellac ocean

But: Like Richard Francis Burton dressed as a Dervish
         this sea dog kept turning around and around
         but never settling down yet everyone said
         he was the most likeable and ordinary of men

But: Back onshore he dropped his pants
         in front of a girl so they seized and locked
         him away like a ship in a bottle
         He argued for his compass his sextant

    :   Let out he lay low and this time he found
         nowhere else to go but all the same he went
         No message was called no bottle was found
         his sloop rolled over and down he went

A Cannoli Maker's Second-Person Selfie Metaphysic

Post-God voices of you complained: there were so many of you
there were none. And, pre-God, there was less than one of you.

That's a hard call. That's a stern said. Back off in the beginning
colloids of an all-or-nothing exploded you. How scary are you?

The Dough-maker's hand was poised, unseen in the shadows.
Then as tactile: alarmingly, quarkily, scrolling and shaping you.

A life-hand a touch. Retreating into the dark. But you became
a baker, the endless maker of same things. Of all people, you!

Your life was repeatedly you. By which of yous it must be said:
you, meant as the many, these infinite and brittle shells of you.

But you nightmared. The hand became a hologram, in a fist of
conundrum. Deep in Freudian, nature-nurture, spacey-lost, you.

Still, shells with wet insides. The ultra-sounds show two lines
a pattern, a tireless hand, your genome-own of replicating you.

Androgynous, cannoli spin in space. The male, the female, the
embryonic (or undecided) meta of the many and a single you.

This poem a Kubrick not a Rubick spin. It needs your name,
your seal in the dough. Your 'all of us'. Our un-youing of you.

Variations and Mutations of a Seduction

1
out on the lake
a man rows with a woman
past trees and weeds their genomes
tangled and as different as Bosch
on his face. he wants.

on Friday on this lake
he wants to seduce her
and so he seduces he pays
whatever it takes.

the swans stay distant.
the water like tin the diagrams dim
two-dimensional him.

she reads her iPhone. she swans.
he silhouettes her in.

2
                              out on the lake the birds and bugs a man
                    on a boat rows with a woman. through the fading light
          on trees and weeds. their genomes echo inside them like trees and weeds.
                    tangled and different as Bosch and Blondie. on the water
                         their figures are want and their figures are dancing.

                    on Friday on his luck on the oars his finger like goannas
          he tries to seduce the much younger woman. he pays he seduces
he pays and he fails. he wants a fuck she wants a fag. he gets no closer
          to whatever it takes. she will empty the water into tomorrow.

               the swans are black but not any closer. on the water's surface
as shiny as tin the diagrams dim. the shadows are swimming the swans
                    too-dimensional. they leave silhouettes.

                    she reads her iPhone her Swanning and Twitter.
                         he imagines her belly her man in a boat...

3

out of luck among birds and mosquitoes one man
in a boat with a woman is crossing the still waters in the failing light.
a hologram of trees and weeds. the genomes echoing. trees and weeds
tungled and deferent. Bosch and Beyonce. he painter she singer. the water
the lap of figures wanting. soon enough small and too late for dancing.

on Friday on the lick on the oars his goanna-like fingers. on hers
slim as a dancer's. he tries to deduce her much younger woman. but imagine.
when he pays for the boat on the day and he fails. no fuck no fag no closer
to whatever. night approaches as day passes. Ever the water into tomorrow.

the memory's black swans are not ever closer. on the water's surface on
light-shifts like tin. his mind is dam the shadows are buts and too many ands.
her womanly lap the shadows are swans the sils and the ohs and the -ettes.

The ex of returning. she swans on her iPhone, the night under water
apes two silhouettes, her ban in a boat … his grinning her groaning.

4

                    The luck of mosquitoes! the bugs and the beetling.
                    one man one boat and across from a woman. his failing.
              no hologram, no genomes! their echo ! their trees and their weeds
          too tungled and different. Bosch is Beyond him. he handful she water.
              whose lap are they in? their large and small too lost for dancing.

                    on Friday. his iguanas are blistered are licky. and dim
                as a chancer. he wants to reduce her her signification. she feys
          and he pales. no fack and no fug. no closer whatever except to *whatever*.
                              night is approaching.

                              his swans? her laughter? on the water's
                    light-shifts like tin the mud of his diagrams dam.
                         beneath the water the sadness of swans.

              her strong X his weak Y. he row and he gunnel she shingle
                    and grunning. her belly, her ban her man in a moat…

5

as cold as a lake's wet. they are returning.
the man in a boat and a woman.
onto the shore her echo
is ghostly. she is laughing
and he is lost.

his fingers are blistered.
his pain is tomorrow his painful reducer.
whatever she imagines
is soon approaching.

sadder than swan light. flat shadows
of them. dire and damn. he steps out
and drags the boat up.

his shingles. his plan. her ban.
her X it. his Y.

The Care of Old Rope

Listen to this you landscape poets.
Old engine parts are a nature scene. Indoors.
What a load of old rope: Jeff Walls' Rembrandt-laden
photo of beautiful mess.
Nerve-shocks of syntax, fluorescent globes.
Everything I've collected en masse for forty years
stacked in one room, everything
garish or grey, shapely, in and from the dismal
or special ... with one seat
park-benched somewhere near the southern white
cliff of the gallery.

I want to crouch on it and win
the Turner Prize. Thoughtfully. Thank you, thanks,
it is an honour. This my life flashing before
your eyes, yes, this is all my junk:
the happy the hapless
shit and tangle I never threw out. Does it stand in
for me, if so how desolate it is, and I reject it.
Yes, yes, I kept it, but that was
habit not value. Now there is new rope.
Denial is an act of identity. Don't do it.
My other selves on the bench
(unaccountable) clutter.

Before the man in Jeff Wall's photograph
untangles the impressively coiled rope his fascination
(it's sisal and it's blue and it's a shipyard long
and a snake-pit of coils) I go to gather myself
but stop gathering tangle before the tangle
becomes impossible, the job blank,
the mind losing without knowing, all it loved and lost
or pulled through the hands like rope burns
and now could never throw out.
Rendered equal and fibrous. *New* rope.

Very Nearly

What was their marriage like? A modern one.
She was older, he was very young, they had
a girl who budded softly on her shoulders.

Another marriage was traditional, that kind.
He was much older, she was young, and they
had a boy who never spoke, who sang.

Her face was effortless, her mind consumed
the world around her, and when she laughed
she rose above the ground. They saw her.

Nothing worried him, then everything, he learnt
his own condition, it had rules he knew alone.
He never spoke aloud what he imagined.

Her wings were like louvres, golden in the sun.
She was a lyric poet, he was a nature poem, they
were made for each other. They died young.

Shiftwork in the Factory of Snow

The whiteness moves under the roof of my brain.
Before that the snow came in dust like a bakery
over pipes as velvety as the seat of my overalls.
At the centre of the far wall is a big wheel-cock
I am responsible for. It calibrates the night-flow
hours 1am until 9am that are my ghostly shifts
in the machinery room. I'll turn hours a fraction
like a wheel or a software system that allows me
to stop, to wait, to bend my ear to its sound, its
cold conversations, the words men use at work
and forget immediately they go home. But now
the shift is all mine and the snow's dust. I know
there are pipes like worn-out velvet in my chest.
I have a white beard, I'm pale from sleeping daily
for night-shifts: my baggy eyes are long and tired
like my wife's breasts. Come 1am my nerves relax
the hours after nightmare, or day men, the fights.
This factory is very well lit for ghosts and ghosts
prefer that. They like to practise fading in and out
on the snowy wall no one can see a ghost against.
They drink at snow-packed bars of fluorescence.
I felt I knew. So cold now in this factory of snow.
Life's not more if it's less: it's no consolation test.

River in Twos

for my father

The river flows two times and two ways which do not differ
from the water, from the banks, from its suit of turquoise.

Colour is never a river but a principle of rivers and some are
the Blue and White are names of rivers more vivid than yours.

Rivers go where you cannot follow. You take wood and add nails,
to bridge it, above the water, under the blue, the death of a child.

Under the bridge you watched it moving like a game of stones,
like Go. Thoughts, gains and losses, and unlimited deepening.

Disappearing downstream, not the same, its banks, in principle
changed, and you, observing, changed utterly and, yes, the same.

Some deaths ruin us but most do not. Its undercurrents never
change: this was there, is there, will remain there. Your own.

This rises on you like water in running seasons rises against
the piles of the bridge. You can live here with names, or ways.

Each day the bridge is a must — a lifetime of nails into boards
to make two sides meet. There is this. There is always river.

In the house, once a home, in a room, you look up at the clock
as you always did. Then the barometer. Then back to the clock.

Selling the Herd up the Road

Undo the roads from the front gate to the house, these roads
to the sheds, to the dairy, the down-hill and across roads.

The sensory roads of the strongest smell and least of directions
a cow has learnt, all the hard-underfoot and the soft roads.

The roads not-made at all the roads inside the ear and shunting
of the blood where roads are not but walking makes them roads.

Shin-echoes as knocked-down by hoofbeats in summer and mud
ways slippery in the wet, habits of stepping and invisible roads.

Every road except the last road inside the crate, the cattle-truck-
road, not that, but the roads in and the flying-up-in-dust roads.

No mass is said on them, and nothing ominous or portentous.
Without new ceremony, and without old, they are empty roads.

The no-cows walking-on-them. Under slow water and the sun
ironed in silence over them. The hundred-cattle-years of roads.

Twos

Then: as a child I could track and fetch back an animal lost between
two lines of a walking cow-ghazal. At the river — hoof-prints in twos.

Now: these two lines are the one found and fetched thing that I
know best from closer practice, and the cows are my forever lost.

But I remember them. I can see them spread out beyond the two
tracks in the gravel-stanza they made as they left. I remember that.

The gravel road forty years later still unsealed thanks to the stubborn
councillors who don't live on it, our farm a last and only destination.

Then: the cows made their one last trip walking in their two-side tread
from the back-worlds of paddock and shed and the scented pastures.

To another farm they are gone. And we walked back along the roads
they this one trip trod two tracks in but all the names of the cows gone.

I imagine this. I was not there, but I remember the other cows walking
to cattle-sales and gone. Cows have their eyes set forwards, heads up.

I am not there. My brothers are sick. Cancer has walked along through
both of them. They cannot walk back to the farm as they remember it.

Cows don't farm farmers. But their broad heads and hips can farm
a deep music, of Now and Other. They are the beautiful elephants.

Two for Tim

for my brother Tim

And Then, You Said What It Was Like

Our tractors started on petrol: to heat up the iron block
of the engine until power-kerosene burnt hard and clean.

A glass bowl under the tanks filled from wheel-taps
fed the metal line of petrol through to the cylinders.

Driving off we'd lean out like side-car men reach to
gravity and turn off the petrol, turn on the kerosene.

Cleaning the bowl, once, the line flooded raw kerosene
down my wrists and onto the bare inner skin of my arms.

I washed it off fast. But kerosene is faster and it burnt
for hours its paining red gloves up to my elbows.

Without symptoms, random leukaemia turned you cold.
The power of your working life stopped, taps turned off.

And on: as you watched the nurse in gloves and green
protective apron setting up the drip: chemo in a clear sac.

Full, but then for hours, down its see-through lines, its
slow emptying. And then, you said what it was like...

We're not close. With our different volatilities we
burn differently, but the shock of your metaphor

returns: that pain on my inner arms and veins,
and your brain and body *filling up with kerosene.*

In and Out of the Body

Removed from what he was by illness. Infection
waits like language, like reading, a syntax inside him.

Moving nowhere far, just in case (it stops waiting)
he reads strange books that a farmer might never read.

Books with no sensible knowledge, no plans for irrigation,
no herd improvement (the herd gone), books closer to pain.

He reads strangeness in its own language, words and images
new yet old … amnesic almost. Books of no easy knowing.

Books of facts where the facts are suppositional, but serious.
The reader ceases adding it up, but it adds, and it increases.

And of different persuasion, a reception not a judgment.
He knows a man may be beside himself by reading.

He reads Kokoda, his hands hard and his eyes soft, from
our father's quiet returning (no logic to dying or surviving).

Seeing in photographs the passing, the sentences of hoping
onwards, like remission. The ambiguities of medicine.

The story not over, the story never clear, the blood cells'
little metaphors: the bus routes, the detours, the terminus.

Cape Lilac: What the Boy Said

Lilac
as a sounded lyric made a primal shift.
And the tree spread hugely above him
its green leaves and mauve-knit stars
cortex of lilac.
Its hooting scrambling stadium of parrots
or small people or atoms its electron shell
wing and breast and blossoms in barkish
lichens knotted and scabbed its branches
up-rushed him thirty metres. Oxygen tilt
of the gap gasp his head filling with dreams.
Lilac
the pixellated word he stood uplifted in.
One tree meant more than any number
or length of universities.
So in a smaller lilac he
built a wood-and-bag cubbie in half-forked
off-slung branches he smoked cigarettes
stolen from his father he read
books of the *ferweh* not the *heimweh*.
Above him and inside him the travelling.
Lilac
was a rising chute he climbed up into
he was crazy he was not of the world
when slung into it all his blood left him
for it. When he came down
                    the canopy collapsed
him. His legs changed him back
into the boy of him.

Shorts

Courage
and H. pylori

Now there was a brave man:
Barry Marshall drank the future
dissolved in a dose of warm bacteria.
On the third day there rose in him
an awful swarm of ulcers.
So then he drank the past
in the form of antibiotics.
He was made good again.
This guy wasn't make-believe.
He did what he said.

Metaphors

An hour after the accident his right hand
became - resembled is not a culinary term -
Szechuan ribs in sticky red sauce.

Surgeons worked on it for hours and made
it into a baseball mitt – of that same hand –
he had to stand behind the plate.

We were feeding carrots to a donkey
when it chomped my toddler's hand.
You can't pull away, or shout enough.

The doctor said: they are rubber, immature
bones, they compress but rarely crunch.
They were as soft as my shame.

Even Shorter

I thought hard
and my thoughts lay
like heavy ropes on concrete
I looked at them hard.
They began to move
like pythons.

*

She tells me
the two women
are as alike as eyebrows
but one is hungrier.

Odour

His father burnt his favourite toy
and stood unsmiling in the room.

As if all abuse has a smell
a smell it's remembered by.

*

I hadn't known about sex
because sex hadn't arrived

But Eric told me this man
had taken his pants down

Then sucked on his cock
Eric didn't know but said

The man smelt worse than
the toilet this happened in

Alterity

At home he spreads cellophane
on the dining room table, smoothes it out
then crushes it, watches it uncrackling,
hating its return, crushes it again,
its crenellated crackling.

He is one thing at a time. No view but one.
His lungs are crackling in the darkness, his
brain - waits for her like black cellophane.

Natural Selection

No matter his own brilliant game
only when the better player wasn't playing
would they pick him in the team.
Fame is a cruel captain.

A study claims to show anxiety levels are between 20% and 70% lower in people who have had Botox

Facing Into It

I met a man whose forehead smiled
more than his face. I saw a man whose
forehead broke on a reef in the middle.
He was a killer. It's hard to forget a face
like that, or the forehead. Or of Putin's
dead-soul face and the paradox of his
tit-pout lips. How they break on a table
and twitch and shout all the way down
to where his frightened Generals sit.

Not Summer

His face is like heavy rain sliding down a window.
But he's a summer man!
He can't unhear it telling him he's sad.

Mirror Mirror

Mirror me before I see: your glass is a scene
without edits, not life, not film, no credits.

So you make me have to decide: do I want
more of what I am, or less? Can I even tell?

You go before me, my superior, my satirist,
and your cool sense of humour. My jowls

are falling for you! Before then, the plain
face of not-here not-here again, not sure as

you and I in this small room after the steam
has left the mirror clear ... We were lovers

only in having such intimacy. I never could
go further, cold mirror! Allow as then I was

this face you never tire of looking at.
But I am unfaithful, I always look away.

Inheritance

When your face arrives it isn't what you ordered. What's it mean?
But too late for returns. Not that I ever do them.

It wasn't a contract you signed. I'm a brain and battery I am your
control room (stand-in for God) of being not of meaning.

Now I'll never leave. I remember the best and worst of things
too. I am a pessimistic epigene. The sins of the father.

The sins of the mother. The codes and coma, every bit of data
and delusion. The hot and cold and fattening seasons.

The hunger ... the alms. I am never one for a few-drinks-in
nostalgia. But some of you has entered me. I've changed.

Didn't you know? You died a little, micro-chimera, and quick
as a fish, a tiny cell, you spawned in me your ghost.

But I live in you as watermark, when you're held up to the light:
hello : the face you see is the face you lost.

Anger-Man (not a superhero)

The man in my face
who threatened me

If blood is as blind
anger is a junkie

What else is worth it
when nothing works

not punching my face
ruins his self-esteem

The man will return
wronged to do wrong

If nothing works to fit
wrong into its return

Fear of the man's anger
makes returning worth it

Fear is not a junkie
or what else is a man

A wronged man has
no limit if he wants

The day until he comes
back to get whatever

Assuages it and then if
he punches and I fall

Unheroically do not rise
then *I* will know his limit

Seeing Gallipoli From the Alterworld

This new religion, pushed by politicians, of ANZAC.
C.W. Bean who told the tale but wasn't there to see it.
Shellfire mythologies can backfire. Now it's revealed
our Private Simpson performed 'no conspicuous act'
of bravery. Only braving chance: with his back turned,
as hundreds of other bearers we have never heard of,
who are, alike, dead. Simpson had a pretty good trot.
His donkey might have won a VC when men did not.
It was in fact requested. Lost to myth, an out-of-hand
insult to numberless men and women, who in war as
in peace, enlist in Status Quo, are buried and forgotten.
Simpson's upward face, Donkey's shaggy downward.
Flapping bravery made of canvas and of slow rumour
from cliff to beach, tracks like war-stained bandages.
War is abstract before and is manipulated after. But
no dash into no-man-and-his-donkey's land? No 300
critically injured men on creaking trips to the beach?
Just Simpson singing (and his donkey braying?) back
turned to machine-gun fire, small ink-blots in the hair
and khaki, spreading like rumour. Simpson, his lightly
wounded soldiers sharing tracks with the other silent
Christ-like bearers, their faces lost, bodies lost, names
never once mentioned nor Mentioned in Dispatches
as Simpson's was. We can bear to love one character,
and suffer his death, like poetry, a particular entering
our general. Then forget the general for the Private.

West Gate Falling

On this bridge the workers did not stop as one man
stopped, and held, who thought to hurt his wife
meant throwing her daughter from the bridge.
Forgetting, like the young man with the knife
and his wife's child in his lap, the child
was his own child. These sick men, of their
self-vasectomies: the trauma of being men
greater than their own children.

The bridge where 39 workers still working plunged
held above water and mud, between concrete
and air, heavy-feathered by the sound of bolts
snapping like river-birds, calls yearning above water
at dusk. They must have thought of wives and kids
or family or lovers or anyone they hugged
once or more, they could never know the future
of that man making so sad their bridge.

Their own fall was into the newspaper chutes
opened and spread the next morning, nothing
saved them, knowing their name, family, children.
Not last thoughts, long afternoons as the footy
kicked life through them, or guilt, or debt, their guises
lost in falling. Known by a kind word to a child
on the pavement outside the house or by singing
raucously over the barbecue at Xmas, gone
from them into the air they were leaving.

Beneath a sad bridge is the grief's held breath.
Water moves on its sad tides as slowly as music.
They fell into the same fear, perhaps like a child,
falling into why and wind-roar, the traffic of air
speeding the heart and slowing the light
as if sensation is all of everything there is.
Tiny, a daughter. Or thirty grown men. Falling.
No time for questions.
Nothing like answers.

Time and Motion Study: Last Rites

Death of a Dog

Perhaps a snake
untangling in the rocks
or the shockable neighbours
or she trimmed a jogger's ankles
or from something equally shrill she
was bitten or baited.

She was a silly and disobedient
dog as a character actor given the
same few roles: eating hoses digging
howling at decibels indoors. When she wasn't
lunging onto furniture or vomiting on rugs
she was a lovely happy idiot of a dog.

But now she is a side-walker
a crab-style or trying-to-tango star
until the up-curve of her back makes us
think she's hit a car (her verbs are active)
until she wobbles and is merely drunk.
She collapses on the bathroom floor.

Characters are better in anecdote
than lived with. But she stands and falls
and props (the vet, by phone, says she must
be poisoned, and gone) in fever stiff her
nose hot on something but her eyes
suddenly cool compelling for the first
time in her life. Tense as Butoh

she stares as if *we* are dead dogs.
Or she stands on a cliff edge all flat
surfaces and sudden drops. Her claws
scratch into the slate floor her last
dog signs. So death is the one thing
she listens to. And she does as she
is told: she knows how to die.

Abattoir

Glare falls from rows of sky-lights
onto the jumpy rows of animals
no light anymore they are solid
non-light they're black red white
the hammer or the gun for cattle
the boofy headphones for pigs
packed in the race more bloody
customers he yells out to a mate
and dreams of a cigarette then
stunned slit a smile if not quick
they are dead and gone they kick
the skinner or the head-cutter a
leg muscle jerks but it's memory
without a rememberer or retreat
enters a room of steam and stink
like a drycleaners in a madhouse
their stomachs spilling the mash
grain of stars or gut emptiness
of the night in the yards for men
in white cloth caps and knives
moving in and back in Tai Chi
reaching up to universal energy
and pulling it down the brutal
chainsaws shoved into gnashing
at man-height the men stepping
lost in the body and womb-wrap
sawing down until its swinging
clear the spine twins apart each
a fist and thumb and little finger
extended like a curse over these
who work in rhythm like blood
inside its territory and the pigs
in one piece move in pale suits
the bearded men in plastic skirts
through a brief peace where they
drift smoothly along in time to
each grunt of the chiller door.

Duck-season

Duck-season is the time for ritual: men abandon cars
at farmsides, roadsides, riversides, roadmap on the dash,
spare cartridge belts, red thongs — spares of worship.
Men wading or prostrate in mud, fearful of only one thing:
meeting brother snake, the tiger - where they are trespassing.
Night is pumped out by shotgun, shells smoking
over forearms; the darkness is buckshot with stars,
the water is delicate with tiny down, parachutes of
pin-stars. Ducks die of the tiniest holes. Only
night feels the bleakness and morning sees the sacrifice
of no-sightings: swans with shattered wings, shags
without necks, dabchicks in bloody huddles, beaks
smashed like mussel shells. Drifting downstream.

Time and Motion Study: Eels

If or when you have gone your life has
gone with you lost in the numerical flux
that disowns us all. So if thinking back
is impossible, then all your life that was
is impossible. But ... you try to imagine
swimming vigorously upstream - an eel
is glassy from the warm Pacific currents
turning over in impossible remembering
unwilling to let it go. Your primal habit
is power because of its unknowing, but
you yearn to feel its habitat around you.
Force yourself, a living thing, upstream
to where you have a middle life and go
not to spawn, but to find what you left
in words like the shimmering nutrients
flashing clarities you wrote or thought
finding anew what you hadn't yet done.
Not a river of regret, but of retribution.
Fast and slow water are barely noticed
when you are the speed and navigation
around you, under tightening surfaces
where branches stop you and you must
swim under and around your decisions.
Glass eel you are exposed like early birth
your inner self visible: spine and feeling
organs, until hunger turns you a yellow
changeling, yes, but for what? To swim
in the night's deep chords, the current
wrapping around you, elver, not yet eel,
but eel-longated, your eel-thighed leap
into shifting light rain sun over swoon
of you becoming one, the sky a chute
you must resist entering. Down again
to dodge hooks and nets the predators
you will survive like the shark-crowns
of teeth, now you read surfaces of stones
with your lips, the shallow mossy curves

you kiss and leave slipping through gaps
at last into open waters. Into backwaters.
This, now, its great nothingness, its rest,
for your overwhelming unknowingness
to exist.
                        But again and for what?
Like an afterlife before your life is done?
Where you might forget everything, this
eating and eel-as-sybarite, its wet Lethe
of world-time continuing without you,
yes, to *laze* as an adult for decades as if
in a coma, a long eel comma on a long
phrase of becoming, the swooning you
later won't be able to remember better
than as pleasure. But is an eel even eel
at all unless you have turned eel silver?

There is no better way to say this. The
beginning and the middle and the end
are not untrue, not mere conveniences
to knowing, but there: entirely wrong.
You were leaf-like in oceans as spawn
then glassy, then yellow, then, wait ...
the hedonist alive in bliss is forgetting
everything and what you forget is not
anything but a possibility, some attempt
no god and no genius enters or protects
until you become again muscle, purpose
and only now Eel. Back downstream
go overland if you must - and you can
because that is how you came, if true
knowledge is now the end as your life
was luxuriant, now out into the ocean
heading north to somewhere unknown
you are as lover and you are gendered
and you spawn. You are an artist, Eel.
No one knows you, not even you know
you, what took you away, what brought

you back, and nothing of what results
from it, if when from nothing nothing
comes. Your Eel heart visible now, you
can be seen for what you are, oceanic.

Acknowledgements

Some poems from this collection have appeared in the following publications: *The Age*, *Antipodes*, *Australian Book Review*, *The Best Australian Poems 2007* ed Peter Rose, *Cuttlefish* ed Roland Leach, *Unfurl 5* ed Stephen J Williams, *The turnrow Anthology of Contemporary Australian Poetry*, ed. John Kinsella, *The Keeper of Fish*, Puncher & Wattmann 2011. My thanks to David Musgrave and Miranda Douglas for the design and publication of this book. The cover image is from a Hologram Flow sequence thanks to YouWorkForThem (www.youworkforthem.com)

www.ingramcontent.com/pod-product-compliance
Lightning Source LLC
Chambersburg PA
CBHW031005090426
42737CB00008B/685